WELCOME TO

My World

Do you remember the time?

BAD

they say the skies the limit
and for me that really true
But my friends you HA ve Seen Nothing
Just wait till I get through because,

I'm BAD
I'm BAD
come on
you know I'm Bad I'm BAD
you know it,

To order the entire "Bad" hand written lyric as a numbered lithography from the strongly limited Michael Jackson collection, send an e-mail to lyrics@michaeljacksonshop.com for further information.

BLACK OR WHITE

Don't Tell me you agree with
me when I SAW you Kickin DIRT
in my eye,
   But iF your thinking
Being my BABy iT Dont matter
iF your BLACK or white.

My you think of Bein my BROTHER
it Dont matter if you Born

   OOH OOH
   YEAH YEAH YEAH
its BLACK it white it tough FOR
you To eat that its BLACK MeetsWhite
OOOH

HOW DOES IT FEEL?

When I am on stage, I feel comfortable. That is because there are always hundreds of thousand people that come to see me and my show and that is one of the greatest emotions a human being can feel, I think. I feel their love and love them dearly... not only my fans, but all people.

Although you are a very popular person, you have success and you are known around the world there are times in which you feel very lonely. Very cold inside. Your mind and your soul is freezing. I am crying a lot. Especially when you know that there is so much love in the world, and there are moments in which you just can't reach out. You are lonely and left outside alone.

In 1994 I wrote "Stranger In Moscow" - a song about a very difficult period of time in my life. It was difficult not only because of what was going on actually, but I was very lonely for a very long time. *I* was freezing.

I was wandering in the rain
Mask of life, feelin' insane
Swift and sudden fall from grace
Sunny days seem far away
Kremlin's shadow belittlin' me
Stalin's tomb won't let me be
On and on and on it came
Wish the rain would just let me

How does it feel
When you're alone
And you're cold inside?

Here abandoned in my fame
Armageddon of the brain
KGB was doggin' me
Take my name and just let me be
Then a begger boy called my name
Happy days will drown the pain
On and on and on it came
And again, and again, and again...

Always love.
~ Michael Jackson

SMOOTH CRIMINAL

And they came in
thru the out-way
It was Sunday
What a black day

Every thought was
out to find him

A R y OK
R y OK A

BILLIE JEAN

Billie Jean

she WAS more like a beauty Queen from a Movie
scene I SAID DON'T MIND but WHAT DO you
mean I am THe one who will Dance on the floor
in the RanD

Billie Jean is NOT my lover she's just a
girl that claims that I AM the one the
KID IS NOT MY SON, She SAYS I AM
the one the KID is noT My Son.

YOU ARE SO BEAUTIFUL

My fans are the reason why I continue to do what I do. I see them as my family, my friends, my children.
I am not the same man without my fans. I dedicate this book to all of you and want you to know how much
I love you all.

You are so beautiful, to me.
Your true love showed me the way
The way I had to go
I walked with you

A thousand miles
through hurtful lies
Standing strong with you
Fighting this all through (so through)

You are so beautiful
You are so colorful
You are just magical
You are salvation
to me.

Your near dried my tears
washed away all my fears
The hole in my soul
was covered up

Because you ...
You are so beautiful.

(You are all that I am)
(Deep In My Soul)

You were there.
~ M.J.